SHOUT TO THE LORD!

CONTENTS

ISBN 0-634-02241-5

HAL•LEONARD® CORPORATION

7777 W. BLUEMOUND RD. P.O. BOX 13819 MILWAUKEE, WI 53213

PREFACE

Although I wrote this collection of arrangements in the summer of 2000, I really have been preparing these settings over a number of years. I often improvise on these themes during church services, fashioning an offertory out of "El Shaddai" or a rousing postlude from "How Majestic Is Your Name." These praise choruses have proven to be favorites in my home church, and I'm sure many of them are loved in your congregation as well.

Writing this book has been a labor of love for me. Each one of these songs has been meaningful in my life and holds a special memory. My hope is that you will find these settings useful in worship services, recitals, piano festivals or in your quiet moments at the piano.

Sincerely,
Phillip Keveren

BIOGRAPHY

Phillip Keveren, a multi-talented keyboard artist and composer, has composed original works in a variety of genres from piano solo to symphonic orchestra. Mr. Keveren gives frequent concerts and workshops for teachers and their students in the United States, Canada, Europe, and Asia. Mr. Keveren holds a B.M. in composition from California State University Northridge and a M.M. in composition from the University of Southern California.

AS THE DEER

Words and Music by Martin Nystrom

As the deer panteth for the water, so my soul longeth after Thee.
You alone are my heart's desire, and I long to worship Thee.
You alone are my strength, my shield; to You alone may my spirit yield.
You alone are my heart's desire, and I long to worship Thee.

You're my friend and You are my brother, even though You are a King.
I love You more than any other, so much more than anything.
You alone are my strength, my shield; to You alone may my spirit yield.
You alone are my heart's desire, and I long to worship Thee.

I want you more than gold or silver, only You can satisfy.
You alone are the real joygiver and the apple of my eye.
You alone are my strength, my shield; to You alone may my spirit yield.
You alone are my heart's desire, and I long to worship Thee.

This is one of the finest examples of the magic that occurs when a wonderful lyric and inspired melody come together. I have tried to assist the gradual build of this arrangement through the use of modulation, but the intrinsic beauty of the composition lies in the soaring melodic line. We sing "As the Deer" frequently in my church, and it has become meaningful to people of all ages.

PK

AS THE DEER

Words and Music by
MARTIN NYSTROM

EL SHADDAI

Words and Music by Michael Card and John Thompson

El Shaddai, El Shaddai,
El Elyon na Adonai,
Age to age You're still the same,
By the power of the name.
El Shaddai, El Shaddai,
Erkahmka na Adonai,
We will praise and lift You high,
El Shaddai.

Truly a contemporary classic. This arrangement begins with four-part choral writing, slowly opening up into a flowing pianistic interpretation. "El Shaddai" utilizes a harmonic progression that is reminiscent of the classical tradition, so I wanted to maintain that spirit in this setting. This piece has become a staple of my piano repertoire, and it lends itself well to improvisation.

PK

EL SHADDAI

Words and Music by MICHAEL CARD
and JOHN THOMPSON

Andante, in reverent chorale style

GIVE THANKS

Words and Music by Henry Smith

Give thanks with a grateful heart,
Give thanks to the Holy One,
Give thanks because He's given Jesus Christ, His Son.
And now let the weak say, "I am strong!"
Let the poor say, "I am rich because of what the Lord has done for us!"
Give thanks.

A university composition student of mine, Jeremy Irish, was the first to point out to me the shared harmonic progression between "Give Thanks" and Pachelbel's "Canon in D." It seemed a natural combination. I was preparing a Christmas concert at the time, and I immediately began work on a piano arrangement. Since then, Jeremy penned a woodwind quintet for his and Elinor's wedding utilizing this idea as well. I believe you, too, might find this piano setting ideal for wedding ceremonies!

PK

GIVE THANKS

Words and Music by
HENRY SMITH

D.S. al Coda

CODA

HOW BEAUTIFUL

Words and Music by Twila Paris

How beautiful the hands that served
The wine and the bread and the sons of the earth.
How beautiful the feet that walked
The long dusty roads and the hill to the cross.
How beautiful, how beautiful,
How beautiful is the body of Christ.

How beautiful the heart that bled,
That took all my sin and bore it instead.
How beautiful the tender eyes
That chose to forgive and never despise.
How beautiful, how beautiful,
How beautiful is the body of Christ.

And as He laid down His life
We offer this sacrifice
That we will live just as He died:
Willing to pay the price, willing to pay the price.

How beautiful the radiant Bride
Who waits for her Groom with His light in her eyes.
How beautiful when humble hearts give
The fruit of pure lives so that others may live.
How beautiful, how beautiful,
How beautiful is the body of Christ.

How beautiful the feet that bring
The sound of good news and the love of the King.
How beautiful the hands that serve
The wine and the bread and the sons of the earth.
How beautiful, how beautiful,
How beautiful is the body of Christ.

I heard this song the first time as a vocal solo in a worship service. I was stunned. I immediately went out and found the Twila Paris CD. It remains one of my favorite songs. I spent a great deal of time on this arrangement, searching for the right combination of rubato, lyricism and drama. I hope you enjoy this setting.

PK

HOW BEAUTIFUL

Words and Music by
TWILA PARIS

With tenderness, freely expressive

With pedal

GREAT IS THE LORD

Words and Music by Michael W. Smith and Deborah D. Smith

Great is the Lord, He is holy and just;
By His power we trust in His love.
Great is the Lord, He is faithful and true,
By His mercy He proves He is love.
Great is the Lord and worthy of glory.
Great is the Lord and worthy of praise.
Great is the Lord; now lift up your voice,
Now lift up your voice:
Great is the Lord!
Great is the Lord!

It seems appropriate to approach this great song in a stately manner. My arrangement borrows heavily from the stylistic language of the baroque and classical periods. It would be effective to take a somewhat slower tempo at measure 36, returning to tempo primo *at measure 43. I would also take the coda (m.56) at a brighter tempo, maybe not* presto *or* vivace, *but certainly with vigor.*

PK

GREAT IS THE LORD

Words and Music by MICHAEL W. SMITH
and DEBORAH D. SMITH

With stately grace

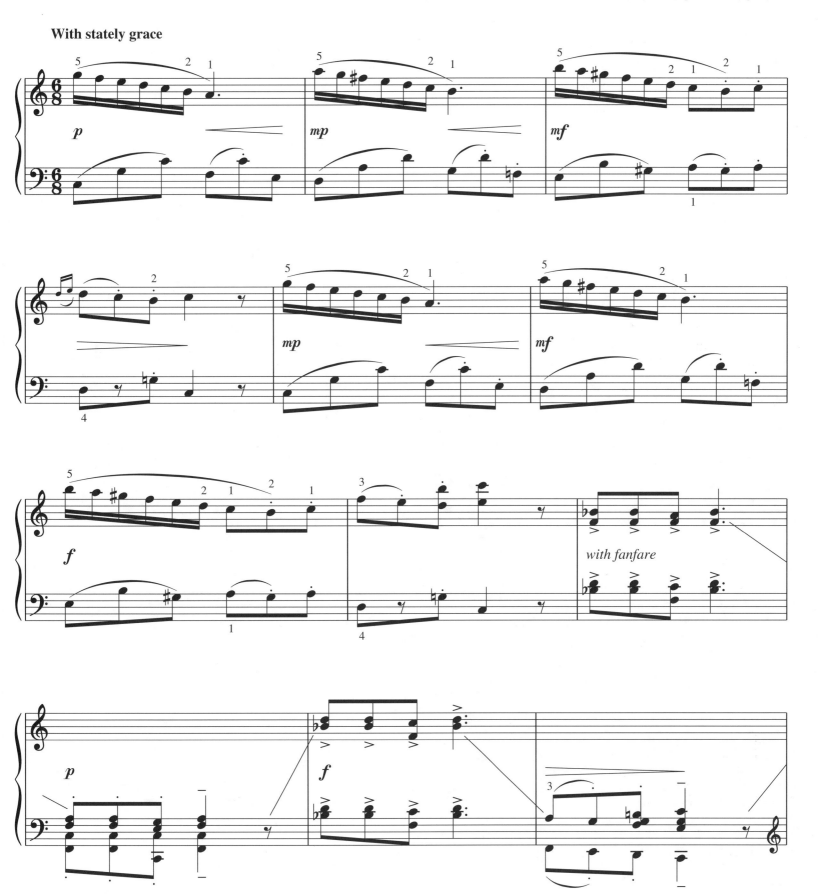

HOW MAJESTIC IS YOUR NAME

Words and Music by Michael W. Smith

O Lord, our Lord, how majestic is Your name in all the earth.
O Lord, our Lord, how majestic is Your name in all the earth.
O Lord, we praise Your name.
O Lord, we magnify Your name:
Prince of Peace, mighty God,
O Lord God Almighty.

My approach with this arrangement was quite orchestral, bringing the majestic colors of the symphony to the piano. The introductory fanfare should imitate brass and timpani. Lighten the touch at measure 9, thinking of harpsichord and strings. Since this chorus is so well known, I elected to take some license at measure 36, varying the theme and time signature. I believe this setting would work well for a worship service postlude.

PK

HOW MAJESTIC IS YOUR NAME

Words and Music by
MICHAEL W. SMITH

Triumphantly

Allegretto

LORD, I LIFT YOUR NAME ON HIGH

Words and Music by Rick Founds

Lord, I lift Your name on high,
Lord, I love to sing Your praises.
I'm so glad You're in my life,
I'm so glad You came to save us.
You came from heaven to earth to show the way,
From the earth to the cross, my debt to pay;
From the cross to the grave, from the grave to the sky;
Lord, I lift Your name on high.

This song has captured the imagination of congregations everywhere. It is at once simple and profound. I decided not to imitate a contemporary worship band, but to place the theme in a classical landscape. It will sound best at a bright tempo, keeping the touch crisp and articulate. Play the melody with more lyricism in the waltz section (m. 49). Make the transition between time signatures (m. 91-92) seamless, with no change in tempo.

PK

LORD, I LIFT YOUR NAME ON HIGH

Words and Music by
RICK FOUNDS

MORE PRECIOUS THAN SILVER

Words and Music by Lynn DeShazo

Lord, You are more precious than silver,
Lord, You are more costly than gold.
Lord, You are more beautiful than diamonds,
And nothing I desire compares with You.

I have heard many arrangements of this beautiful song over the years. My favorite treatments have been simple and direct, mirroring the unadorned nature of the melody. This arrangement starts with the delicate simplicity of a music box, gradually varying the melody and building to a climax at measure 43.

PK

MORE PRECIOUS THAN SILVER

Words and Music by
LYNN DeSHAZO

O HOW HE LOVES YOU AND ME

Words and Music by Kurt Kaiser

O how He loves you and me,
O how He loves you and me.
He gave His life, what more could He give?
O how He loves you;
O how He loves me;
O how He loves you and me!

I heard this sung by Evie Tornquist when I was a young, aspiring musician. Her vocal performance was exquisite. The piano accompaniment was perfectly tasteful. It touched me deeply spiritually, and it confirmed my desire to become the best musician I could be. I cannot remember if the performance I heard that night used "Jesus Loves Me" as an arranging motif, but I've heard it many times since then. This arrangement makes use of this device.

PK

O HOW HE LOVES YOU AND ME

Words and Music by
KURT KAISER

SHINE, JESUS, SHINE

Words and Music by Graham Kendrick

Lord, the light of Your love is shining
In the midst of the darkness shining;
Jesus, Light of the World, shine upon us,
Set us free by the truth You now bring us,
Shine on me, shine on me.

Shine, Jesus, shine,
Fill this land with the Father's glory;
Blaze, spirit, blaze,
Set our hearts on fire.
Flow, river, flow,
Flood the nations with grace and mercy;
Send forth Your Word, Lord,
And let there be light.

Lord, I come to Your awesome presence,
From the shadows into Your radiance;
By the blood I may enter Your brightness,
Search me, try me, consume all my darkness,
Shine on me, shine on me.

CHORUS

As we gaze on Your kingly brightness,
So our faces display Your likeness;
Ever changing from glory to glory,
Mirror'd here may our lives tell Your story,
Shine on me, shine on me.

CHORUS

This chorus is very powerful in congregational singing. I wanted to make it "sing" in a unique way on the piano, so I chose a semi-classical approach to this contemporary song. This arrangement would be especially effective in a recital setting.

PK

SHINE, JESUS, SHINE

Words and Music by
GRAHAM KENDRICK

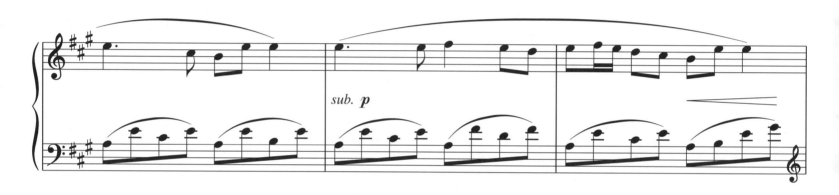

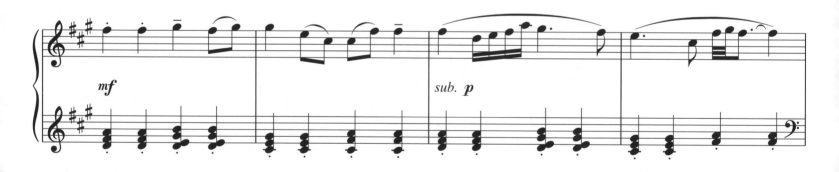

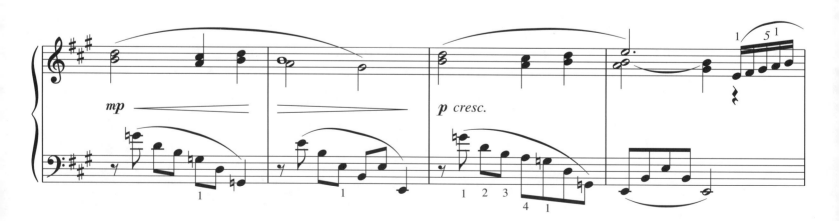

OH LORD, YOU'RE BEAUTIFUL

Words and Music by Keith Green

Oh Lord, You're beautiful,
Your face is all I seek,
For when Your eyes are on this child
Your grace abounds to me.

Oh Lord, please light the fire
That once burned bright and clear,
Replace the lamp of my first love
That burns with holy fear.

I want to take Your Word and shine it all around,
But first help me just to live it, Lord.
And when I'm doing well, help me to never seek a crown,
For my reward is giving glory to You.

Oh Lord, You're beautiful,
Your face is all I seek,
For when Your eyes are on this child
Your grace abounds to me.

Keith Green left us some musical gems. This is one of them. The bridge is not often sung in congregational settings, but is included in this arrangement (beginning in measure 43). The left hand accompaniment figure established in the introduction needs to be light and smooth.

PK

OH LORD, YOU'RE BEAUTIFUL

Words and Music by
KEITH GREEN

Gently flowing

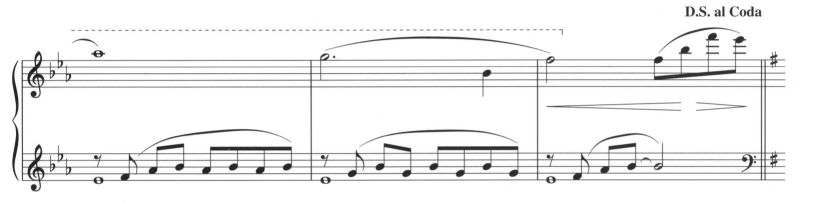

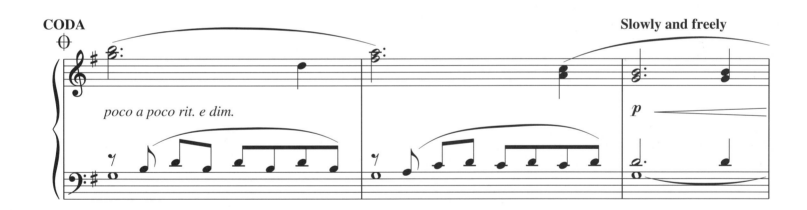

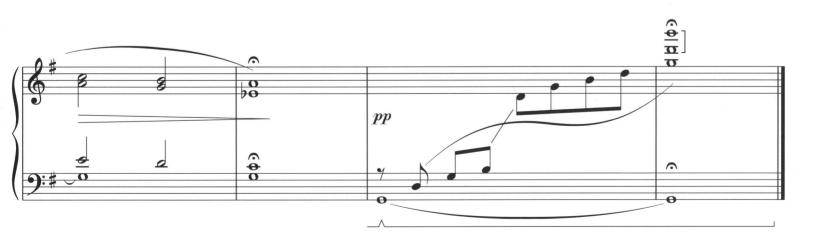

A SHIELD ABOUT ME

Words and Music by Donn Thomas and Charles Williams

Thou, O Lord, are a shield about me.
You're my glory, You're the lifter of my head.
Hallelujah, hallelujah,
Hallelujah, You're the lifter of my head.

Based on Psalm 28:7, this chorus has a majestic quality that always moves me. I heard this song the first time while on retreat. I am transported back to the mountaintop whenever I hear it. The contrast between the sweet lyricism of the verse (m. 9) and the powerful resonance of the chorus (m. 25) makes for a stirring solo.

PK

A SHIELD ABOUT ME

Words and Music by DONN THOMAS
and CHARLES WILLIAMS

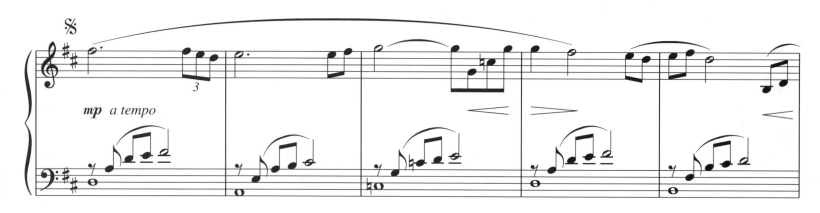

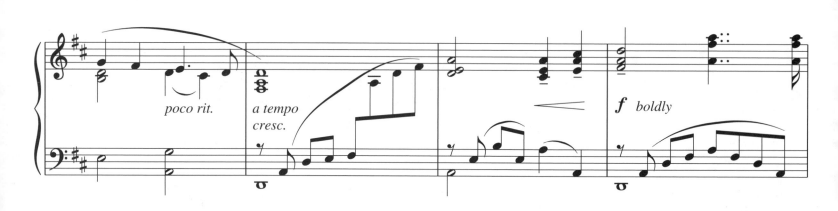

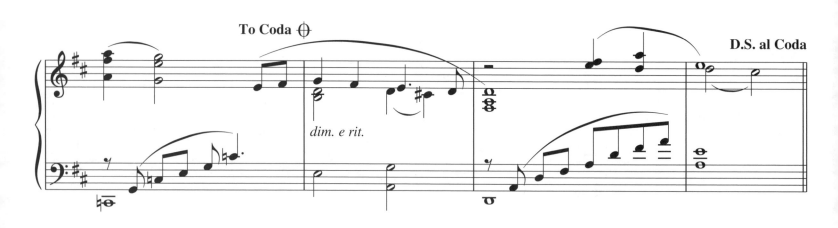

CODA

SHOUT TO THE LORD

Words and Music by Darlene Zschech

My Jesus, my Savior;
Lord, there is none like You.
All of my days I want to praise
The wonders of Your mighty love.
My comfort, my shelter,
Tower of refuge and strength;
Let ev'ry breath, all that I am
Never cease to worship You.

Shout to the Lord all the earth. Let us sing
Power and majesty, praise to the King.
Mountains bow down and the seas will roar
At the sound of Your name.
I sing for joy at the work of Your hand.
Forever I'll love You, forever I'll stand.
Nothing compares to the promise I have in You.

It is rare when a song speaks to so many people so powerfully. This is one of those great songs that reach out to young and old alike. To me, it has a similar impact to that of mighty hymns like "How Great Thou Art." I approached this setting in a pretty straightforward manner, trying to get out of the way to let this magnificent song shine through.

PK

SHOUT TO THE LORD

Words and Music by
DARLENE ZSCHECH

THY WORD

Words and Music by Michael W. Smith and Amy Grant

Thy Word is a lamp unto my feet
And a light unto my path.
Thy Word is a lamp unto my feet
And a light unto my path.

When I feel afraid, think I've lost my way,
Still You're there right beside me.
And nothing will I fear as long as You are near.
Please be near me to the end.

CHORUS

I will not forget Your love for me, and yet
My heart forever is wandering.
Jesus, be my guide and hold me to Your side,
I will love You to the end.

CHORUS

As a harmonically rich composition, "Thy Word" lends itself beautifully to a Mozartian setting. This arrangement features a short development section (m. 23-28) and some thematic variation beginning in measure 29. I believe this piece would serve well as a recital or festival selection.

PK

THY WORD

Words and Music by MICHAEL W. SMITH
and AMY GRANT

Allegro con moto